My Love And Life:
IN BLACK

By

Michael Black

ISBN: 0-75963-528-5

This book is printed on acid free paper.

1stBooks - rev. 07/20/01

ACKNOWLEDGEMENTS

I want to first thank the good Lord and my Savior, Jesus Christ, for the talent, ability, and the desire to share and help develop talent in others, especially the youth. I would like to thank my family, Eric, Chris, Stanley Black and Beverli "Sunasia" Anderson for their love support. I would also like to thank my mom, Betty Black-Dickerson, for her undying love and belief in me along with her contribution for this project.

I obviously cannot thank everyone I know, personally, But I would like to thank everyone of my childhood friends in Freeport, New York and my hang out buddies in Hempstead and Lakeview-Malverne and all the young ladies we befriended along the way. (DDT's you know who you are!) My life would not be complete if I didn't thank my college buddies from Morgan State University in Baltimore and my Pan American World Airways co-workers in New York and Miami. I have to send a shout out to my friends from Bell South in Miami and my current co-workers from SouthWestern Bell in Dallas, Texas as well as all my relatives worldwide!

I also want to wish the Dearly Departed a fond fairwell, as they will live on in our memories forever. My Father, Ernest Black, my nephew Batik Black; Michael Rice, my cousin, Uncle George, Uncle John, Aunt Rose, Aunt Margaret, Grandma Rose and Granpa Herman, Grandma Tessie and my childhood friends; Brian Smith, Charles "Neck" Bennet, Ponchitta & Celita Pope, Baldy Vailes, Wayne and Louis Patrick, Warren "Woo" Wells, Barbara Dangerfields daughter, Felicia and Howard Tompkins sister Che Che. I did not forget you Jerome "T.T." Gates as you were one of my closest friends and I apologize for missing your funeral.

Otis Saunders, Lois Jones, Cleo Thompson, Fred Bryant and my good friend, Clarence "June" Beckford Jr. May God keep you all, Amen.

Thanks to Leslie Tucker at "The Perfect Word" in Baltimore, Md. for your help and support. Special thanks goes to my Pastor Zan Holmes and Pastor Tatum of St. Lukes United "Community" Methodist Church in Dallas, Tex. As well as my entire church family. Thanks for your guidance and support. In closing, I'd like to thank my love and inspiration, Ms. Ruby Ross, for your love and caring: patience and devotion. I love you. I cannot close without giving praise to my Lord and Savior, Jesus Christ for showing me that he is real and he is here for all of us with love and forgiveness. May God Bless You!

TABLE OF CONTENTS

Love: On the Love Side

Hey Girl
Paradise
Sweet Stream
To Love You
It Would Be So Nice
Loving You
One Day, Who Knows?
My Love
Don't You Know That?
A Ray of Happiness
Mystical Magical
For You, My Darling, Everything
Just As You Are
The Moment
How Are You, Baby?
The Journey
The First Time
The Ebb And Flow
I Need
My Love Will Take You There
Sweet Nothings
May I Take Your Order, Please?
MMMMMMMMMMMMMM...
Silent Love

The Downside: of Life and Love

The Upside: of Love and Life

It Wasn't Like
Times
I Really Wanna
Sleepless And Restless
Come Fly with Me
You
All for the Wonder of You
If you Really Want to
Basketball, Parties and Girls
The future is You
Hey Little Girl
Just One touch
Excuse me Miss...

<u>Loneliness</u>

This Shell of Loneliness
Sunrise
Missing Her
I Need my Princess
I'm not Sad, I'm Lonely
I Wish
I'm Lonely Now
Alone Again

<u>Giving Praise: On The Prayer Side</u>

I'm Gonna Live my Life
Now That I've Found you
Praise God
Smile
Before we met
Please Keep your love pure: A Tribute

Observations

Equal Time:
Poems and Prose from my Mom Betty Black-Dickerson

Michael Black

LOVE: ON THE LOVE SIDE

Michael Black

Hey Girl

Hey Girl
You render me helpless
with your stare
You're sexy and you move me
but I can't tell you where
In your eyes are the skies
And your tears
hold the grace and the fears
of a thousand Black Queens
All gently tucked into
Those very tight jeans
is a lady who I have yet to know or care
only to held captive
By that stare
And the lips
That hesitate to part and yield
A glimmering smile
well dipped in sex appeal
So as I part your hair with my fingers
And lift a smile from your cheeks
with a kiss on your chin
I beg those eyes to let me in.

THE JOURNEY

For true love
I'd never surrender
I've waited and waited
for God to send her
and now she's here
I know the journey can begin
to know each other
outside and in
Inside and out
I'd never make
my princess pout
If she did
I'd have to make her
shout it out
But laughs and smiles
Are all we hope to see
one day I'm going to love you
and you're going to love me.

THE FIRST TIME

The first time we kissed
I knew right then and there
you touched me like I've
never been touched...anywhere
and the light
from your face and your smile
has shown
me to a place and to a love
that I've never known
I have to see you
Baby
I have to know
If we can be friends first
Before we let our love go
I have a feeling
Baby
I have a feeling
That happiness was what
your eyes were revealing
And true to you, I'll be
It's so easy to do
With all this love
and a woman like you.

THE EBB AND FLOW

Just like the tides
That ebb and flow
so does my love go
It flows forever slow
my clock's wound too tight
I move way too fast
And I'm in it, quicker
Than a New York minute
But because I'm fast
Doesn't mean I don't need love
or you're not the one
I'm dreaming of
I want you with me
wherever I go
so I can love you
like the Ebb and flow.

<u>PARADISE</u>

Through the wind
my thoughts fly
Higher than a Bird
In a clear Blue Sky
And I wonder why
Through the misty morning
She strolls
Beckoning out to me
And in my sleep, I roll
And fall from sight
Through the night
She awakens me, so nice
A pure and gentle sister of Sugar and Spice
she's paradise
In her eyes lay shades
of Blue love and Red passion
And one day Beautiful children
We will fashion
All our own.

SWEET STREAM

In a sweet stream
Of a summer dream
I swim
'cause heaven is of no sorrows
only tomorrow's
And to complain...
would be to raise a question
You see
Heaven is a place
of Love and tranquillity
And Inferno is the Den
of Malice and Hostility
So I swim to the land
of eternal Love
In hopes that who I'm thinking of
Is there......Alone.

TO LOVE YOU

To Be Myself, To Exist
And thrive amongst the cosmic mist
Is my desire
To share your mind
To seek rare love and to find
Is my life's fire
To love you
is to be
A crystal image in ecstasy
Which no man can deny
Why?
Well, to love life is the start
And a life of love will never part
to be true at heart isn't corny
the coolest ones are always horny
Don't fear my words of obligation
let them touch your heart
And create sensations
let them ease you in your
times of need...
to satisfy loves greed.

<u>IT WOULD BE SO NICE</u>

It would be so nice
to see you again
to hear your voice
to see your smile
And then
we'd have to do something special...
Like
take a romantic walk in the park
sit down and talk
until it got dark
Because I could never spend
too much time with you
And I feel
that I could spend my life with you
Because I want
everything you're showing me
it's true
it would be so nice
to fall in love with you.

LOVING YOU

Loving you is all I see
And your love is what I want
most definitely
You see
I want you every night and every day
Forever
in every and any way
As a friend, Lover
And one day a wife
to love and cherish
for the rest of my life
And more than that
I want you to love me
with love, forever, insatiably
with trust and virtues
That protect like a roof
and a love so strong...It's Bulletproof
As a man, They don't come any better
I come out smiling Through any kind of weather
So loving you is all I see
And In love is how I want us to be!

<u>ONE DAY, WHO KNOWS?</u>

Just sitting here in paradise
Palm trees, Parrots, and the weather's nice
Blue skies all year round
mangos and oranges
on the ground
green, green grass and Blue green water
nice schools
for little sons and daughters
I'd love to have you
sitting here with me
one day, who knows, we'll see
If not
Maybe I could fight the cold
'til my hair turned gray
and my bones got old
and our kids got old
But our Love stayed new
Because Princess
I'll always love you true.

<u>MY LOVE</u>

My Love
My emotions run so high
with thoughts of you so Deep...
I sigh...
In the past I got
Beat down by love
Beat stupid
I thought Mike Tyson was cupid
But now
I'm free to pursue
True Love
And that's what I'm gonna do
with love in my heart
And you in my life
I'll cherish you
My love, my wife.

DON'T YOU KNOW THAT?

Don't you know that feelings grow
and all I know is pain is out there waiting.
Don't you know that life goes on
and so do songs and love: It keeps me dating.
Don't you know that now you're here
and so am I...lets try to get together
Don't you know that time may pass
But love will last and last through any weather
Don't you know that I love you
and you love me and you're my one and only?
Don't you know that I have fears
and fears make tears without you
I'd be lonely?
Don't you know that tears they fall and fall
and all and all the while they glisten?
Don't you know that lips speak words
But words Don't feel and feelings never listen
Don't you know that?

A RAY OF HAPPINESS

Through sunny days
and hurricanes
Through dancing fields
of sugar cane
Through roses red
and violets
My love, sweetheart,
keeps calling you
It calls to tell you
of it's quest
to find your heart
and build a nest
to grow, to flourish
and to mesh
our hearts together
in happiness
So if you're out one cloudy day
and the sun should deliver
you a ray
of happiness
just be content
to know the joy my love has sent.

<u>MYSTICAL MAGICAL</u>

Mystical, Magical
Woman
You are to me
Chocolate fantasy
Just for me
with a twinkle in your eyes
like the stars in the heavens
everything you do
keeps coming up sevens
In you
I love everything I see
mystical, magical
Love for me.

FOR YOU, MY DARLING, EVERYTHING

As A Dreamer of Dreams
And a maker of means
I'll give you love
And more than you've ever seen
'cause as a giver of gifts
I have only one wish
That you never want
As long as you live
And if you do
I'll pull the stars from the night
And form a cluster ball of light
And place it on your finger
a ring
For you, My darling, Everything.

JUST AS YOU ARE

Just as you are
is Right for me
It's hard to improve
on perfection, you see
I might Be mad for you
You should be glad for me
It feels so right, so true
How could we ever Be
Any other way
So stay, starlet
And twinkle like a star
So I can love you
Just As You Are.

<u>THE MOMENT</u>

The moment I saw you
My world stopped spinning
My heart started smiling
My mind started grinning
And everything seemed
to be frozen in time
And I was praying
one day soon
you'd be mine
The vision of you
came kind of frantic
I really wasn't ready
to be romantic
I had to regroup and get straight
I had to be ready to troop
for this Date
And I hope Deep in my heart
Before it all ends, It starts
The love of all loves
the beat of all hearts
One Hundred Thousand men
couldn't pull us apart
With God in heaven and cupid here
I'm keeping you very, very near.

HOW ARE YOU, BABY?

How Are you Baby?
How do you do?
How has the world
been treating you?
How was work?
What did you do today?
Did you study?
Was your exam today?
I've been thinking
and hoping
that time would fly
so we could get to know each other
better than a passerby
when I hold your hands
and look in your eyes
I want to kiss you
and hope to never see you cry
you're special
and you're important to me
I'd like to love you in a way
to make you want to love me.

I NEED

I need your loving arms to hold me
your loving lips to never scold me
your loving eyes to see me through
I need to be loving you:
I need your loving smile to send me soaring
your loving voice that's never boring
your loving hugs will always do
I need to be loving you!

MY LOVE WILL TAKE YOU THERE

If you dream of me
And call my name
I'll surely hear it
And if you ever get
to taste my love
You will revere it
True love
will make you walk
through the rain
without a care
And if you don't believe it
my love will take you there
If you wish upon a star
I'll make it all come true
Cause everything you want and need
Is waiting here for you
And if you ever need a hug
I'd squeeze you everywhere
and if you want to know true love
My love will take you there

<u>SWEET NOTHINGS</u>

Although you're far
I hope you're feeling I'm near
I'll send my love
With sweet nothings
That I'll blow in your ear
And the fire thats inside me
Seems to rage in my heart
And the kissing that you're missing
Means we're still miles apart
So please be patient
Have sweet dreams
And have no fears
I'll send my love
With sweet nothings
'til I'm holding you near!

<u>MAY I TAKE YOUR ORDER, PLEASE?</u>

May I take your order, please?
How about I order you
with some Beluga caviar
and some cognac too!
with a hot tub or jacuzzi
Just off from a blazing fire
champagne and rose pedals
Before we retire
Just sitting here and seeing you smile
would be enough
without the fire or the roses
or the rest of that stuff
But wouldn't it be nice
with all that stuff, too?
A back rub in rose pedals
it's all up to you!

<u>MMMMMMMMMMMMMMMMM...</u>

When I close my eyes
I can still see your smiling face
The wonder of your love
Awakens me with each embrace
As I Dream and Dabble
with what could be
I prepare
for my next encounter with thee
Now, I know a good woman
can appreciate a good man
who's sensitive
and can love you like I can
and kiss you
so you'll never have to miss
everything you want
and a love like this!

<u>SILENT LOVE</u>

For you
my silent love
cries out
never would I dare to shout
never could my lips reveal
The warmth and tenderness
my heart feels
The passion rages on
As though in a storm
with only thoughts of you
to keep me warm
Lovely thoughts of loving
You're all I'm thinking of
The Beautiful Passion
of Silent Love.

<u>THE DOWNSIDE: OF LIFE AND LOVE</u>

Michael Black

DO YOU THINK...

Do you think
I could control
The rage
The passion of the soul
Burning Deep Down
and out of control?
Do you think
I could be fooled
by childish games
I learned in school?
At your feet
I could place
The moon and stars on a plate
Escort you out
on an all expense Dinner Date
take all the love
I have, for you,
and stop it on a dime?
Every time.

I REMEMBER

I remember way back
when you used to smile
I'd call you and we'd laugh
on the phone for a little while
Do you remember our first lunch date?
We kept going in the elevator
to kiss
and you didn't say wait
you looked so sweet
and I gave you that rose
I kissed you on your cheek
and even on your nose
But now
you don't have time to see me
Not much
your favorite slogan is
Please don't touch
I never used to have to wait
hours when I paged you
the way you looked at me
was like I tried to cage you
and now, I can't even get you on the phone
I guess I'll have to leave you alone.

I KNEW

I knew you had a man
But the relationship
I could not understand
a voice so sweet
turned my heart from meat
to fluid tear
I laughed and lied
But deep inside...I cried
a girl like you
could have made all of my dreams
come true
but you took my heart from my chest
my mind from my brain
and left me with the shame
of a bully turned lame
I felt bad...and I died.

LOOKING BACK

We've come so far in life; us two
It's amazing when you think
About what we've been through
like life
we take the good with the bad
and cherish the fond memories we've had
with good friends and neighbors
naughty deeds and capers
Always on the run
And all in the name of fun
Sometimes it's nice to reminisce
About the past loves who've passed the tests
and others who time did forget
and yet...though life and times have passed
Them by...sometimes its good to cry.

WHEN WE LOVED

When we loved
You couldn't stick a pencil
In between us
So much happiness and joy
You should have seen us
Life was so full
So full of love
Everytime I looked to Heaven
I saw a dove
When we loved
Every sound had a song in it
And no matter what I did
There was no wrong in it
We always laughed and kissed
At the drop of a hat
It was truly heaven
Just to live like that
We did things for each other
Because we wanted
Our house was a happy home
But now it's haunted
Everytime we talk
We always seem to fuss
Smiles turned to frowns
Joy to disgust
Now you're lying to me
And I'm not trusting you
If we can't get back to the love
We're through!

<u>INCREDIBLE</u>

Incredible as it may seem
my tale is reality
and not a dream
for my pride, I suffered
and not for my jewel
when she left me to choose
between proud man and fool
and since my jewel
was not my wife
and with my pride I must live
for the rest of my life...I left
her actions spoke of disrespect
selfishness and neglect
and she wanted me to forget?
To forget the pain
and to forget the shame
If I would have stayed.

LIFE SAVER

My life is so dim
I can hardly swim
In the sea of vitality
My minds in a moat
where it can't float
on the surface of reality
I need a lifesaver
A woman who won't waiver
Under the stress and strain
of my emotional pain
A woman who can afford to give
some joy
In my quest to live
Happily ever after!

A TRAGIC LOVE TALE

This is a tale
Of love and sorrow
Yesterday they loved
But they both feared tomorrow
When they kissed
And held hands
Everything was alright
But the love was short lived
As It crept through the night
And It pushed them apart
And created distrust
Then the fear and the doubt
Seemed to rise through the dust
All the love that they had
Couldn't keep them strong
The days and nights
Never seemed so long
And just when love
Could have saved the day
All the evil came in
And drove the lovers away!

<u>THE LAST GASP OF LOVE</u>

Loving words
So full of joy
Now, must seem so hollow
Even belief in me
Must be hard to swallow
I'm like a love bird
Without a love song
Where did we go wrong?
(How can this go on?)
One moment of displeasure
Ends it all in despair
The arms that held the future
Are up in the air
The eyes that held a champion
Now seem to look right through
What am I to do?
(This time I'm dumping you!)
Things could be alot better
But they couldn't get worse
One minute I'm in heaven
Right now I need a nurse
I don't even want to have to
Mend a broken heart
Why do we have to end?
(We need to be apart)
And all the time
I ask myself
What does it really mean?
Was I really that bad?
Could love not intervene?
How can you take your
Love from me
And say that you still do?

How can you take the sun away
And light come shining through?
How can you look in crying eyes
You loved
And still say <u>no</u>?
Please, I have to know.
(Um, I have to go.)

MEN CRY TOO, SO WHY DON'T I?

I know I have a heart
But why can't I feel it
No matter the pain or sorrow
I can't reveal it
When most can't take it anymore
I just sigh
Men cry too, so why don't I
I know I have it in me
But it just won't come out
When faced with something really sad
I only seem to pout
I'm sure if I could shed
one tear
Others would surely fly
Men cry too, so why don't I?

Michael Black

<u>THE UPSIDE: OF LOVE AND LIFE</u>

Michael Black

IT WASN'T LIKE...

When we met
It wasn't like we hit it right off
from the start
or
we couldn't keep our bodies apart
I mean
we weren't like Anthony and Cleopatra
and all night
I can't stop looking atcha
you know
It wasn't like
a lot of romance
I mean
you wouldn't even slow dance
but this is now
and that was then
you'll never hear
that story again!

__TIMES__

Times like these, I could breeze
across the seven seas
and not come down
until I saw the forest...the trees
the birds and bees
me and my honey
living lavishly
and every day sunny
like today
the sun...bouncing off my smile
to permeate my soul
and drive my spirits wild
you know
Reality isn't always cold
There's lots of sunshine
before you get old
yes
Times like these are a breeze
and together
may we see a million of these.

I REALLY WANNA

I really wanna get to know ya
I have so many things to show ya
We have so many places to go
and People to meet
and
so many exotic foods to eat
and
I really, really think
that you're
really, really cute
and sexy and sweet
and classy to boot
and I'm going to try to do
every little thing I can...
to be your man.

SLEEPLESS AND RESTLESS

Sleepless in New York
are you thinking of me?
are you aroused or
is it the humidity?
Is it moans and groans
that join your sleep?
Is it ecstasy
That your dreams keep?
Is it me, the one who
craves for you
Keeping you up all night
'til a quarter 'til two?
Now I believe
the things that you say to me
'cause I'm restless too
'til a quarter 'til three!
So sleepless in New York
meet restless in Miami
The man who can't even
fasten his 'jamies
'cause in my sleep
I'm calling your name
So sleepless meet restless
we're both the same.

<u>COME FLY WITH ME</u>

Can I take you off to a foreign land
Wine you and Dine you
like only I can
Serenade you under moon and stars
Do lovers lane in Rental cars
Zip you Back to a golden Beach
in Miami
And a Beach like South Beach
And when you get tanned
we're off again
to the Poconos
until you tell me when
You're tired
of all this Love and Affection
coming at you
from all directions
I'm sure the same's
In store for me
Because Darling
You're the one for me!

<u>YOU</u>

You're like a flower
with dimples
you give me goose pimples
all over
You're like a four leaf clover
and I'm hoping and praying
Our friendship you won't be delaying
Now, I'd like to see you
when I can
and you know
I'd love to be your man
someday
I'd really like to see us
get together
I'll bet we'd be like
birds of a feather
and you know
I'm loving the way
you're making me feel
It must be
all that sex appeal.

<u>ALL FOR THE WONDER OF YOU</u>

When I'm alone
I toss and turn 'til two
I sleep like a baby
When I dream of you
This love I feel is all I'm feeling too!
All for the wonder of you!
What have you done to me
What did you do
to make me fall so deep for you?
When my skys are gray
Your sun comes shining through
All for the wonder of you!
You're sugar and spice
And everything nice and new
All for the wonder of you
You know, I asked
And all my dreams came true
All for the wonder of you
When we're in church
I'll have to say, "I do"
All for the wonder of you!

<u>IF YOU REALLY WANT TO</u>

Come with me and you will see
A time
That you can only see with me
If you really want to
Be free, with me
and experience ecstasy
If you really want to
If you really want to
We'll share time
that rhyme no poem
we'll go and be gone
until the return of the sun
as we run
and when we tire
we'll rest under a tree
Just you and me!

BASKETBALL, PARTIES, AND GIRLS

Basketball, Parties, and Girls
That was my world
Enter then Intervene
I'm on the scene
No matter where I went
It was all the same
Basketball courts or the girls
I'm packing game
Brooklyn, Bronx, or in Queens
I'm Iverson
Pulling girls from their jeans
I'm silent son
What you don't see, you don't know
I'm on the go
Baddest whip in the show
I'm packing, yo
Once recognized on the court
At Venice Beach
Superstars giving props
for what I teach
Stopped a party cold
with one move
I've heard it told
Basketball, Parties and Girls
That was my show

THE FUTURE IS YOU

Everything you're wanting
I'm wanting it too!
And everything you're needing
I'm ahead of you
If we plant the seeds of promise
Now
Our dreams
They must come true
Tomorrow is the future
And the future is you
First, we make the plans
And then we execute
You can't plant the seed
Before it sprouts the root
With hard work and prayer
I know we can make due
Tomorrow is the future
And the future is you!

HEY LITTLE GIRL

Hey little girl
How do you stay so sweet
from the cheeks on your face
to the toes on your feet?
Do you bathe in honey everyday?
What does an Angel do
with oil of olay?
Like a Goddess
you appeared to me in a Dream
The most beautiful woman
I've ever seen
and an African Princess
you are
with the light in your eye
of an Egyptian Star
and the smile
that could melt my heart on the Nile
so smile
and let the big man rise to his feet
and find out
how the little girl stays so sweet!

JUST ONE TOUCH

Just one touch
Would mean so much
If you touched me
Just one kiss could never miss
Just try it and you'll see
For you, I know, could easily show
The love you have for me
And as for me, it's true
I got alot of love for you
so
Just one touch
Would mean so much
If you touched me
Just one kiss
Could never miss
Just try me and you'll see!

EXCUSE ME MISS...

Excuse me, miss, But do you have the time?
No, No, Not that time
I'm talking about the time
like from eight to nine
When you're home from work
and your feeling fine
But you're all alone with nothing to do
So you get on the phone But you can't get through
Do you know what I mean? I know you do
May I pose a question that may appeal
to your innermost interest?
Would you like to meet a Brother
who's unlike most others
willing to do what you like to do
and enjoy it as much as you?
If your answer is yes
And you do have the time
A compatible Brother
will be by to see you
In time, on time, with time
to spend that time
with only you!

Michael Black

<u>LONELINESS</u>

Michael Black

THIS SHELL OF LONELINESS

It's so cold in This shell
of loneliness in which I dwell
The walls so barren and cold
No one to have and to hold
from this day forward
I have nothing to fear
Just look around
There's no one here
At least, This way
I'll never have to drag her down
with me
on this cold, cold ground
so dismal
this must truly be hell
In this
shell of Loneliness
In which I dwell.

<u>SUNRISE</u>

Another sunrise I awake alone
No mail or calls on the telephone
No visit and no surprises
only greetings from lonely sunrises
Although you're far
I feel you're near
I can almost smell
Bijon on your ear
I can almost feel your gentle touch
As I kiss your picture in my clutch
Alas, sunrise, very soon
I will be happily greeting you
and alone I'll never be
Because my baby is here with me.

<u>MISSING HER</u>

In a land that's filled
with evil and sin
Inflation's as high
as its ever been
Unemployment is up
and so is crime
with murders happening all the time
In a time when all these things exist
I can still find joy
through one I've missed
with a radiance
and a gentle smile
I can see her adrift
upon the Nile
and modest she is
or at least to me
too modest to see what she's done to me
Too pretty for me to want to stray
Too sweet for me to miss a day
we could spend together
In our own little way.

I NEED MY PRINCESS

I feel like a man
on a desert Isle
The days and nights are so long
I can't smile
Days seem like eternity
I need my princess
here with me
when she's on my mind
sometimes I can't eat
I hurt from my head
down to my feet
It hurts so bad
sometimes I can't see
I need my princess
here with me
If she was here
I'd buy the sun
and hide it
for some night time fun
I miss my darling
desperately
I need my princess
here with me.

I'M NOT SAD, I'M LONELY

I'm not sad, I'm lonely
and missing you
my one and only
I've waited for you
so long
Instead of weakness
I am strong
But still
I miss my honey
without you, nothing's funny
No one to hug or to kiss
only my baby to miss
so hurry back
so we can start
This life of love
with arrows through the heart
and we can be
the best of friends
until the very, very end.

Michael Black

<u>I WISH</u>

I wish you could come tonight
to see me
create the ambiance
and kill the TV
sprinkle rose pedals
all over the sheets
your love and mine
and my nights complete
'cause I can take you
to the moon and stars
squeeze a little tighter
and you might see mars
or Venus
I'd never let evil come between us
on a little Ponderosa
one day
I hope to see us
As for now
I only hope and pray
for long nights with you
and very short work days!

I'M LONELY NOW

You know,
I'm lonely now without you
My mind was lost
Until it found you
Far off
In a state of depression
I'm in pain, too
Here with a sad confession
I miss you
And I'm sorry
For making things
The way they are
One minute, we're together
The next; we're far
If there was a way
I could make it up to you
I would
But I'm sitting here lonely now
I guess I should

<u>ALONE AGAIN</u>

I'm alone again
Now what went wrong?
I never crept before
Now I'm in that song
And it doesn't seem to matter
All the stuff I did right
I guess I hit the wrong nerve
And I hit the wrong night
My love is still here
But my heart is broke
And the fire in my heart
Is replaced by the smoke
And the ashes that fall
Couldn't burn me at all
But the moment she left
So did my breath...
And I called and left a message
But she never called back
Everything we've been through
Must have amounted to jack
I guess all good things
Must come to an end
But there's a new beginning
When you're alone again

GIVING PRAISE

ON THE PRAYER SIDE

Michael Black

I'M GONNA LIVE MY LIFE

I'm gonna live my life
Gonna have fun in life
Not gonna be a dud
Like living stuck in mud
Want to see sand and sea
Tropical ocean breeze
And if I want some snow
Off to the slopes, I go
Never make time to pout
Keep your house clean, no doubt
Please give him Praise Above
He taught us how to love
Gonna help someone out
That is what life's about
Don't wait for them to yell
You be the first one there
I'm gonna live my life
Gonna have fun in life
Not gonna be a dud
Like living stuck in mud
Want to live endlessly?
Just pray to God and see
Happiness is his plan
See you in promised land

NOW THAT I'VE FOUND YOU

Now that I found you
The journey can begin
To walk in the ways
Of the Lord without sin
Father
Help us to walk in the ways
Of the rightgeous and the few
And help us to rekindle
our faith anew
When your love comes down
The sun comes shining through
Now that I've found you!
Now that I've found you!

PRAISE GOD

Praise be to God
It's true
I've always believed
he'd lead me to you
at the time of his choosing
he sent me out
to finally find
and seek you out
when we first met
our eyes and our hands
Did touch
my lips couldn't reveal
that we weren't going dutch
I've got to wine and dine you
support and refine you
give you all the love I have
to give in this life
as your friend and husband
with you as my wife
we'll do whatever, wherever, whenever
we feel it
I would tell you more
but my lips can't reveal it.

<u>SMILE</u>

When I smile
I smile a smile
for a while
and when you're with me
my smile gets versatile
Because I'm happy
so happy that I came out here
to be with family
and to find you my dear
and I'm hoping
you're feeling
like me right now
and forever
Let my love keep you warm
in cold weather
In my embrace
with a smile on your face
makes me smile too
God gave me what I wanted...
you!

BEFORE ME MET

Before we met
My life was a blank
And if it's meant to be
I'll have God to thank
And give him praises
For sending me
An angel like you
And yet I know
There's still so much to do
But I'm here
Oh yes
And I'm here for you
With support and love
To see you through
And for you
I'll do
Anything in this world
For the girl of my dreams
Must be a dream girl!

PLESE KEEP YOUR LOVE PURE

African American Women, you have been given a wonderful gift; the gift of love. The love that a mother has for her newborn child was the same love that God had for this world when He gave his only son to save us all. All I ask is that you keep that love free of doubt and indecision; free of temptation and indiscretion. Please keep your love pure!

African American Women
Please keep you love "Pure"
I understand the pain and suffering
You've had to endure
Now as you sit here
Hold your heads up high
No more cries
From tear-stained swollen eyes
You're the children
Of the greatest people
Ever on earth
And it was from your womb
Mankind knew birth
Through out history
You've always made your mark
Regardless, if your skin tone
Was light or dark
You're more beautiful
Than the face that launched
A thousand ships
With all the riches of Egypt
At your fingertips
You're Parks and Tubman
Nefertiri and Cleopatra

You always seem to excel
When the whole world's looking atcha
With sugar and spice
And everything nice at your core
It's your essence
That I do adore
You've come a long way, baby
From scrubbing floors
Day and night
On your knees
Now you're C.E.O.'s
With Ph.d's
And you're doctors and lawyers
And millionaires, too
A black woman's love
Was the first love I ever knew
So keep God in the plan
And I know you will endure
I love you
African American Women
Please, keep your love "pure".

Michael Black

<u>OBSERVATIONS</u>

Michael Black

I'D BE A FOOL

I'd be a fool
to think
I'd ever see you again
for a drink
a chat, a hug
or a seat on my lap
I think I'd better
take a nap
I'd be a fool
to expect
your attention
or a peck on the neck
But I can dream
so what the heck
But I'd be a bigger fool
If I wasn't ready
when you called
I'll be ready
Body, Soul and all!

TAKING TIME

I don't know why
she's taking so long
she's taking her time
and I'm doing fine
But she's taking too long
you see
memories are sweet and sour
and dreams seem to last an hour
But you wake up and
It's only been a while.

THE GAMES WE PLAY

The games we play
can last all day
Through thick and thin
Hate and love
and hurt the ones
we think most of...and why?
To keep your name from shame
You'd play the same game...and why
I say
Let's put our cards on the table
and get into each other
If we're able
If you stop seeing
Tom, Bill and Jack
I'll stop seeing those women
behind your back
Because to be true
isn't such a hard thing to do
If you really want to!

<u>SEXY</u>

You're sexy
and so exotic
you stimulate and Inflate
the word "Erotic"
you captivate
Every heart and soul
That dare
Perception
to behold
Cleopatra
Never stood chance
To dominate
with a single glance
and captivate
Every heart and soul
Young lady
You just broke the mold!

THE WAY WE ARE; WERE, WILL BE?

Come to me and make my life
so one day you can be my wife
and wear my rings and have some kids
like everyone of your parents did
to continue the name
and see the faces
with joy
and one day they'll go places
and meet their mates
and have some kids
like everyone of their parents did
and soon
we're all very old and gray
much too old to run and play
we don't hear too well
and we can hardly see
when you're old it's "what we were,"
and when you're young
It's "what we will be!"

I AWAIT

I await
The test of fate
The encounter
from our first date
in an attempt to eclipse
All the promises made
from our lips
to our ears
to our minds
and then to our hearts
Then the warm feelings
That the fire starts
followed by the response
known as the smile
That's been known to last
more than a while
so I await
The test of fate
'cause good things come
to those who date!

ETERNITY

Eternity...The Blink of an eye
The birth of a fawn
you think you'll live forever
Then your life is gone
All the time
You sit and wait
hoping you'll happen upon good fate
The time is now
To realize
That tomorrow is now
and now is forever
But act soon
Before your ashes meet the weather
And your bones are cold
and your name...Just a memory
one in a Billion...In eternity.

<u>BEING BLACK</u>

To me
Being black
is more than just skin tone
or a state of mind
Being black
means you can be poor
and live in the projects
and still have fun
Because you look for ways
to keep your mind off the fact that
the white kids across town
Drive corvettes to school
and have their own businesses
and we're catching the bus
But we still have more fun
than they do
and nobody trippin
and seeing a shrink
because our parents broke-up
Because
Being black
means coming to grips with a bad hand
But holding on until the hands
get good enough to get out of the game
Being black; looking up 'til you can look out!

HARLEM, NEW YORK

I always loved Harlem
A true black mecca
or motherland
Like an urban Africa
and like Africa
Everyone isn't black
There's Puerto Ricians,
Dominicans and all like that
Central Park
Ends, (starts), in Harlem
Didn't you know?
Don't forget the museums
And the Great Apollo
And the people
There's always nice people
to meet
And we always went, on Sundays,
to Silvias to eat
All the shopping and the history
There's so much to do
Harlem, New York
I'll always love you!

<u>EQUAL?............Free?</u>

We went from negro to nigger
to colored to African-American
How can it be
That we never really went free?
We went from having
chains and shackles
on our bodies to our minds
And when they came off
Only drugs did we find
And man-made disease
With no where to hide
A stench hung low in the air
The smell of genocide
They killed Dr. King
But they couldn't kill his dream
All the mixed babies
Make the racist scream
We went from
This name to that name
But where will it all end
We'll see
We can't be equal
If we can't be free

SPINNING THE WEB

Spinning the Web
The Web we weave
The maze called life
Cannot deceive
or prohibit
truth from permeating
My heart and soul
The halls of happiness
Will be patrolled
By Love
Now and forever
with a touch of class
Exceeding expectations
and love will last
and last.

Michael Black

EQUAL TIME

POEMS AND PROSE FROM MY MOM
BETTY BLACK-DICKERSON

Michael Black

<u>WHERE WERE YOU LAST NIGHT?</u>

Everything between us
is always alright
We never fight or argue
And the feeling is right
So where were you last night?
You know, I paged you
on your pager
And I called you on your phone
Every hour on the hour
But you still weren't home
So where were you last night?
To try to keep from assuming
I try to keep it light
And when the sun comes up
Everything is looking bright
And when I roll over
And reach for you
You're here
My one delight
But when the sun goes down
And you can't be found
I remember the past
And I have to ask
Where were you last night?

Michael Black

<u>A DAYDREAM</u>

As I sit in the sun
fanning with my program
commencement speaker after speaker
followed by the band
I dream of Doctor, or Lawyer
or vocation that's grand
Then reality hits me
As I hear his name called
it's his 8th grade graduation
Afterall.

THE WEDDING MARCH

The rain that falls in spring
The flowers that bloom in June
Tis the season to hum the tune
of the Wedding March
The day has finally arrived
with family and friends by her side
The groom waits at the altar
Humming the tune
of the Wedding March

B B D

Michael Black

I COULD HAVE...

TIME IS FLEETING-
I COULD HAVE-
I WOULD HAVE-
THEN I SHOULD HAVE.

NOW THAT I'M OLDER
I'D BETTER GET BUSY
DOING SOME OF THE THINGS
I COULD HAVE-
I WOULD HAVE-
AND I SHOULD HAVE.

B B D

HOMESICK

SUNNY SKIES AND SANDY SHORES,
PALM TREES SWAYING WITH
BREEZES GALORE.

A SWEET DAIQUIRI WITH IT'S
LITTLE UNBRELLA-

IS SO SMOOTH
AND OH SO MELLOW.
BUT
I MISS NEW YORK!!

                              B B D

Michael Black

<u>RECIPE FOR LOVE</u>

SING A SONG IN YOUR HEART
PUT A SMILE ON YOUR FACE-
ADD A BOUNCE IN YOUR STEP
AND A WHOLE LOT OF GRACE.

STIR IN COMPASSION
AND A LITTLE BIT OF
TEMPERANCE-
A PLEASANT DISPOSITION
WILL MAKE A DIFFERENCE.

B B D

<u>A GRANDCHILD IS</u>

A GRANDCHILD IS THE
LITTLE ANGEL
THAT YOUR
LITTLE DEVIL
PRODUCED.

B B D

<u>SIMPLY STATED</u>

BOOKS ARE FRIENDS
THAT SOMETIMES DECEIVE-
AN OPINION EXPRESSED
JUST TO RELIEVE.

SO EASE THE STRESS,
GRAB A TOME-
IF THAT DOESN'T DO IT,
WRITE YOUR OWN.

B B D

<u>DID YOU EVER</u>

DID YOU EVER WALK IN THE RAIN?
DID YOU EVER RUN IN THE WIND?
DID YOU EVER WADE IN THE WATER
OR TAKE A SIMPLE SPIN-
ON A DRAGSTER AROUND THE TRACK-
OR ROLLER COASTER AT THE FAIR-
WHERE YOUR HEART IS IN YOUR MOUTH
AND THE WIND IS IN YOUR HAIR?

IF YOU HAVE DONE THESE THINGS,
WITHOUT ANY PAIN,
THEN TRY WATCHING YOUR CHILD PLAY
IN A FOOTBALL GAME.
THAT'S LIFE!!

B B D

Michael Black

THE SEASONS

THE COLD WINTRY DAYS ARE WANING.
SPRING RAINS, FLOWERS AND BUTTERFLIES
ARE GAINING.
THE SUMMER, HOT AND HUMID TAKES AHOLD,
AND FALL REMINDS US THAT WINTER
DAY ARE OH SO COLD.
THANK GOD FOR THE SEASONS.

B B D

<u>REFLECTIONS AT SUNSET</u>

As we come to the sunset
of our years
I look back and wonder,
and sometimes, in tears
The foolish things we did
with no thought of others
Adding gray hairs and wrinkles
to our mothers
Then, having our own families
was another phase
given the little children
to care for and raise
And while trying to be perfect
Mistakes were made
but God saw us through
and our debts got paid
So now, as we come to the
sunset of our years
No need for regrets
but thankfulness for the tears

Michael Black

ABOUT THE AUTHOR

Known in poetry circles in Dallas as "Malik," Michael Black could have easily fit right into the movie *Love Jones*, as he loves the open microphone format of performing poetry. He was born on April 7, 1955 in a military hospital, on what is now the campus of Nassau Community College in Long Island, New York. Michael started writing poetry in 1976 when he was just home from Morgan State University and working for Pan American Airways. Originally a graphic artist, he stopped drawing and began writing, an art form in which he found more complete expression. Michael likes to think that his poetry is "emotion driven" and any emotional high or low is fuel for his poetic fire. For fun, he attends sporting events and occasionally will shoot the basketball. He also enjoys shooting pool, bowling, playing cards, and fishing in the sea.